EXPLORE THE
W RLD

SOCIAL SCIENCE

C0-BWW-724

Hunger
Around the World

MICHÈLE DUFRESNE

TABLE OF CONTENTS

PIONEER VALLEY EDUCATIONAL PRESS, INC

WHY IS THERE HUNGER?

Most of the food in the world is never eaten.
Much of it is thrown in the garbage.
So why are hundreds of millions of people
going to bed hungry each night?

Poverty is the main cause of hunger. Some of the poorest people in the world are farmers who live on tiny lots of land in **developing countries**. Their land is too small to grow and sell enough food to make a living. Even though they are farmers, they don't have enough money to feed themselves. They call the time leading up to the harvest season the "hungry season." By then, they have run out of food from the previous harvest and must cut back on meals until the next one.

People living in cities can also be hungry because their job pays too little to buy enough food. Some families have to cut back on how much they eat at the end of the month before their next paycheck arrives.

War and **conflict** can be another cause of hunger. During a war, many people must find new places to live. Farm fields may be destroyed. Food often becomes too expensive to buy.

MORE TO EXPLORE

In 2014, more than **13 MILLION** people had to leave their home countries. Many of them were escaping wars in Syria, Afghanistan, and Somalia.

In some places, extreme weather events like droughts can damage crops and lead to **famine**. Some wealthy farmers pay for an **irrigation** system to water their crops during dry periods. Poor farmers in developing countries must spend hours each day fetching water from far-off places to bring home to their crops.

Many people live far away from where food is grown. Their food must be transported from where it is grown to where the people live. If the roads are in poor condition, it is difficult for the food to reach the people who desperately need it.

HOW CAN WE FEED MORE PEOPLE?

The world's **population** is growing. As each new person is born, we will need more food to feed them. Is it possible that we might run out of food to feed everyone? Hopefully not. Scientists are working on cheaper, faster, and healthier ways to grow enough food for our growing population.

Sunlight provides energy to plants and helps them grow. Most plants use only a little bit of the sunlight that they receive. Researchers are working on ways to help plants use all of the energy they receive from the sun. They believe that plants may be able to produce twice as much food if they can do this.

MORE TO EXPLORE

Plants absorb nutrients from the soil. Some farmers have found a way to mix those nutrients with water, allowing plants to grow without soil.

We already know how to alter some plants to increase how much food they produce. We call these genetically modified organisms, or GMOs. GMOs are designed to grow in very hot places and to resist pests. Because they are easier to grow, they produce food that costs less.

GMO fruits

natural fruits

But there are some downsides to GMOs. They can be dangerous to insects and may threaten the environment. Also, they can leave behind unwanted chemicals in the soil. And the genetically modified plants can easily spread to nearby farms, even if those farmers don't want them.

Some foods are naturally easy to grow. In tropical areas, breadfruit trees produce a fruit that is sometimes called a tree potato. When it is small and green, breadfruit tastes like an artichoke. When it is ripe, it is like a potato. When it is very ripe, it becomes soft and sweet like a dessert. It can also be made into flour or chips. It is high in protein, vitamins, and minerals.

Breadfruit grows quickly without the fertilizers and **pesticides** that rice and wheat need. A single breadfruit tree can produce up to 250 fruits a year. It can feed a family for many years. As more breadfruit trees grow, there may be more food to go around.

HUNGER AT HOME

Hunger is not something that only happens far away. In the United States, one in five children do not have enough to eat each day.

The National School Lunch Program offers free or low-cost breakfast and lunch to children who come from homes where there is not enough food. But only about half the children who need free breakfast or lunch are getting it. Some schools may not have a free lunch program, or meals may only be offered for part of the year.

At some schools, children with unpaid lunch bills receive a stamp on their arm that reads, "I Need Lunch Money." These children may be told to clean the cafeteria tables in front of their friends. Even if the cafeteria workers want to help them, the school may require that they give those children only cold lunches. This is called lunch shaming.

States are starting to pass laws that forbid lunch shaming. The laws require schools to either work with parents who are behind on lunch payments or help them sign up for the free lunch program.

CAN WE SHARE FOOD?

Have you ever thrown out food from your lunch tray that you did not want to eat? Some schools have found a way to share that food instead of throwing it away. Unopened items from lunch trays are left on a shared table. A student who doesn't want their apple or milk can leave it for another student to pick up, free of charge. Shared tables can reduce waste and help children who are hungry.

A study at one school found that nearly 100 whole fruits were thrown away, untouched, every day.

HUNGER GAP

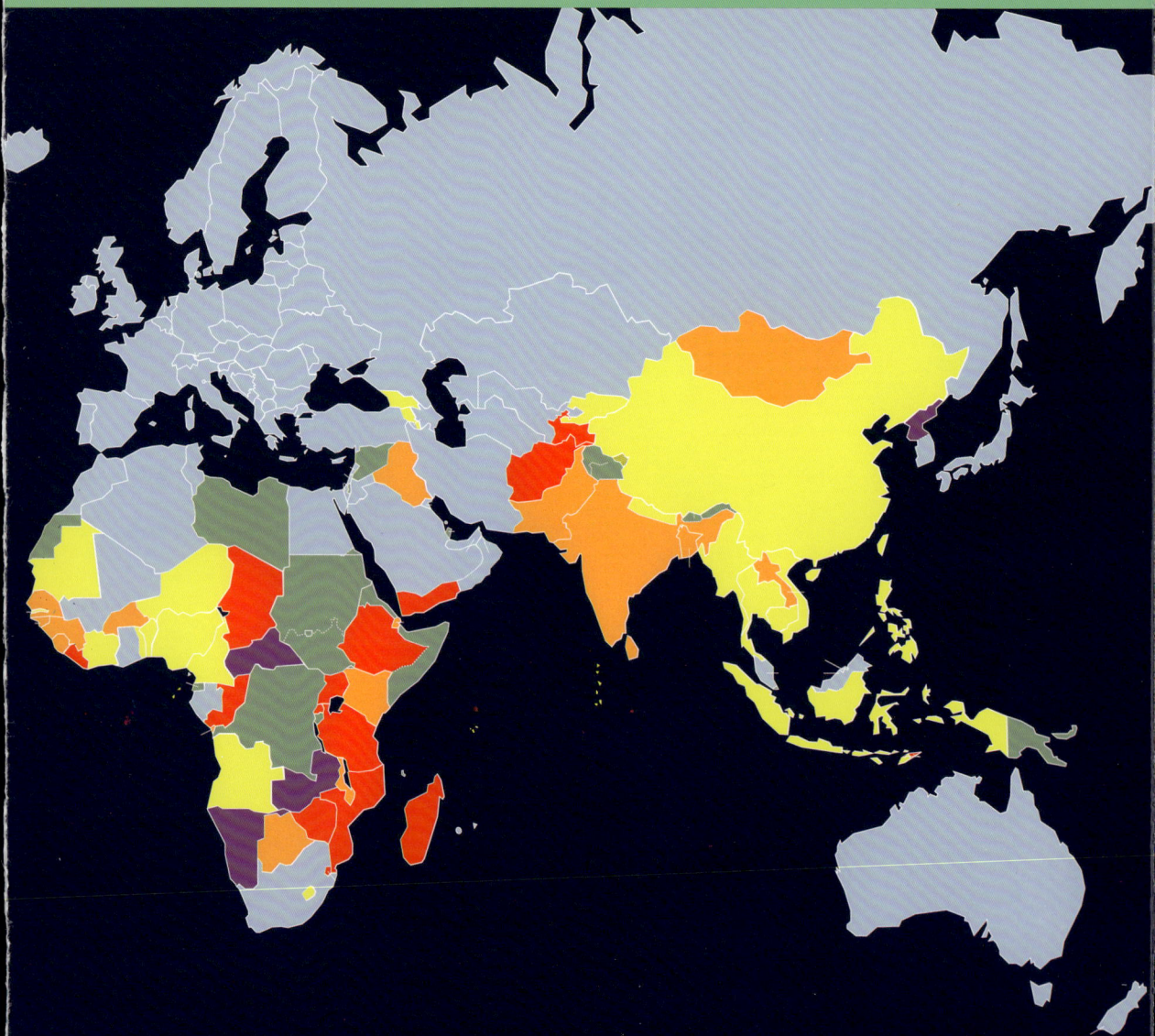

THE WORLD

As of 2017, one out of every nine people in the world doesn't have enough food to eat. This map shows the countries with the highest percentage of people who struggle with hunger.

0-5%

5-14%

15-24%

25-34%

+ 35%

Insufficient data

GLOSSARY

conflict
a struggle for power

developing countries
nations with few industries

famine
a lack of food that causes hunger for
a large group of people

irrigation
supplying land with water through pipes

pesticides
chemicals used to kill animals
or insects that damage crops

population
the number of people in
a certain place

poverty
the state of being poor

INDEX